Daniel Boone

A Buddy Book
by
Randy T. Gosda

ABDO
Publishing Company

VISIT US AT

www.abdopub.com

Published by Buddy Books, an imprint of ABDO Publishing Company, 4940 Viking Drive, Suite 622, Edina, Minnesota 55435. Copyright © 2002 by Abdo Consulting Group, Inc. International copyrights reserved in all countries. No part of this book may be reproduced in any form without written permission from the publisher.

Printed in the United States.

Edited by: Christy DeVillier
Contributing Editors: Matt Ray, Michael P. Goecke
Image Research: Deborah Coldiron, Susan Will
Graphic Design: Jane Halbert
Cover Photograph: North Wind Picture Archives
Interior Photographs/Illustrations: North Wind Picture Archives, Denise Esner, Deborah Coldiron

Library of Congress Cataloging-in-Publication Data

Gosda, Randy T., 1959-
    Daniel Boone / Randy T. Gosda.
        p. cm. — (First biographies. Set II)
    Includes index.
    Summary: A simple biography of the well-known frontiersman, Daniel Boone.
    ISBN 1-57765-735-7
    1. Boone, Daniel, 1734-1820—Juvenile literature. 2. Pioneers—Kentucky—Biography—Juvenile literature. 3. Explorers—Kentucky—Biography—Juvenile literature. 4. Frontier and pioneer life—Kentucky—Juvenile literature. 5. Kentucky—Biography—Juvenile literature. 6. Kentucky—Discovery and exploration—Juvenile literature. [1. Boone, Daniel, 1734-1820. 2. Pioneers.] I. Title.

F454.B66 G67 2002
976.9'02'092—dc21
[B]

                                                        2001034929

Table Of Contents

Who Is Daniel Boone?

Daniel Boone is a famous pioneer. Daniel helped to settle the Kentucky frontier. That was about 225 years ago. Back then, Kentucky was wilderness. Daniel Boone was skilled at hunting and living in the wilderness.

Daniel Boone was born on November 2, 1734. Daniel had a big family. He had 10 brothers and sisters. Daniel's mother was Sarah Morgan. Daniel's father was Squire Boone. Squire Boone was a blacksmith.

Many pioneers lived in log cabins.

Growing Up

The Boone family lived near Reading, Pennsylvania. Back then, this land was on the American frontier. Young Daniel spent a lot of time in the woods. He loved to hunt. Young Daniel hunted with a sharp, wooden stick. At age 12, Daniel learned to hunt with a rifle. A rifle is a special gun.

Daniel learned to read and write. But he was not a good speller. Daniel liked the woods more than school. Young Daniel learned a lot about the wilderness. This helped Daniel become a great hunter.

Young Daniel loved to hunt.

Daniel Boone lived on the frontier.

In 1750, Daniel's family moved to the North Carolina frontier. Daniel liked his new home. This land was full of animals for Daniel to hunt. Daniel earned money by selling beaver and muskrat furs. The Boone family often had fresh meat for dinner.

John Finley

Daniel Boone met John Finley in the British Army. Daniel and John fought in the French and Indian War. John told Daniel stories about the Kentucky wilderness.

In 1756, Daniel Boone married Rebecca Bryan. They had 10 children. Daniel farmed and hunted in North Carolina and Virginia for many years. But he did not forget John Finley's stories about Kentucky.

Exploring Kentucky

Daniel Boone liked to go on long hunting trips. In 1767, Daniel went to the edge of Kentucky. He camped at Salt Springs. Kentucky was full of deer, buffalo, and wild turkey. Daniel thought Kentucky's grasslands would be good for farming. Daniel thought Kentucky would be a great place to live.

Daniel Boone made many trips to Kentucky.

In 1769, Daniel went back to Kentucky. This time, he went with his friend John Finley. Four other men went with Daniel and John. They headed through the Cumberland Gap. The Cumberland Gap is an opening in the Appalachian Mountains.

In 1769, Kentucky was wilderness.

In 1773, Daniel's family tried moving to Kentucky. But something happened before they got there. American Indians attacked them. They killed Daniel's son, James. So, Daniel and his family went back home.

The Shawnee Indians attacked Daniel's family.

The Wilderness Road

In 1775, Daniel Boone started working for the Transylvania Trading Company. This company needed Daniel to clear a path to Kentucky. This path would be the first road to Kentucky. There were 28 men who helped Daniel Boone build this road. Later, people called this path the Wilderness Road.

You can travel Daniel's Wilderness Road today.

CUMBERLAND GAP
HISTORIC PASS
ON THE
WILDERNESS ROAD

The Wilderness Road was very important. Between 1775 and 1795, over 70,000 people traveled Daniel's Wilderness Road. Many people used the Wilderness Road to move to Kentucky.

Daniel helped build a settlement near the Kentucky River. This settlement was Boonesborough. Boonesborough was one of the first settlements in Kentucky.

Daniel's family was among Booneborough's first settlers. People named Boonesborough after Daniel Boone.

The Cumberland Gap

The Shawnee  Indians

The Shawnee Indians often attacked Boonesborough. So, the Boonesborough settlers built a fort. An army guarded the fort. Daniel was the leader of Boonesborough's army.

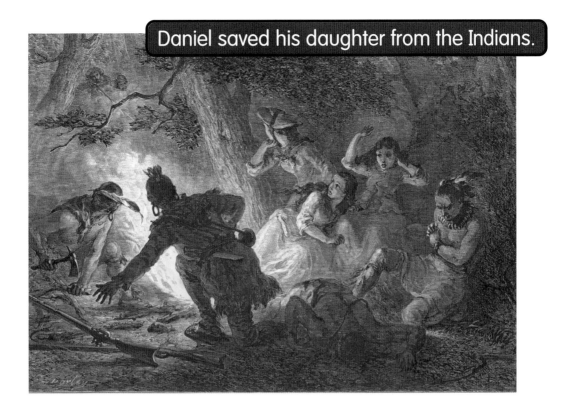

Daniel saved his daughter from the Indians.

In 1776, the Shawnee carried off Jemima Boone. Jemima was Daniel Boone's daughter. Daniel found Jemima and brought her home. But trouble between the settlers and the Shawnee did not stop.

The Shawnee Indians carried off Daniel in 1778. But they did not hurt him. The Shawnee respected Daniel's wilderness and hunting skills. Chief Blackfish made Daniel a member of the Shawnee tribe.

Daniel respected the Shawnee Indians. But he wanted to go back to his family.

Chief Blackfish was a Shawnee Indian.

One day, Daniel heard the Shawnee talking. The Shawnee were planning to attack Boonseborough. Daniel worried about his family. So, he ran away.

Daniel ran back to Boonesbourough. Daniel and the settlers fought off the Shawnee. This battle is called the Great Siege of Boonesborough. After seven days, the Shawnee left Boonesborough.

Boonesborough's fort helped to keep the settlers safe.

Daniel Leaves Kentucky

Over time, more and more people settled in Kentucky. In 1792, Kentucky became a state.

Daniel wanted to live near the wild again. So, Daniel and Rebecca moved to the Missouri frontier.

Daniel spent the rest of his life on the wild frontier. He lived to be 85 years old.

Daniel Boone had great respect for the wilderness. This great wilderness man helped to settle the Kentucky frontier. This makes Daniel Boone a famous American pioneer.

Daniel Boone, a great wilderness man.

Important Dates

November 2, 1734 Daniel Boone is born.

1756 Daniel marries Rebecca Bryan.

1767 Daniel goes to Kentucky for the first time.

1775 Daniel builds the Wilderness Road.

1776 The Shawnee Indians carry off Daniel's daughter.

1778 The Great Siege of Boonesborough takes place.

1792 Kentucky becomes a state.

1799 Daniel and Rebecca move to the Missouri frontier.

September 26, 1820 Daniel Boone dies.

Important Words

American Indians Native Americans, the very first people to live on American land.

attack to start a fight.

blacksmith someone who works with metal to make and mend things.

fort a building with strong walls to guard against enemies.

frontier land that is not settled.

pioneer one of the first people to settle on new land.

wilderness wild land where few people live.

Web Sites

Today in History: June 7
http://memory.loc.gov/ammem/today/jun07.html
This Library of Congress site contains photographs and highlights from Daniel Boone's life.

Daniel Boone Paintings
http://www1.truman.edu/academics/fa/faculty/jpaulding/yadkin.html
Learn about Daniel Boone through this slideshow of beautiful paintings alongside biographical facts.

Index